Loosing The Key of David

Minister's Guide

Stephen Fredericks

Key of David Healing Ministries LLC

Kennesaw, GA

Unless otherwise noted, all scripture quotations are from:

1) New King James Version of the Bible Copyright ©1979, 1980, 1982 by Thomas Nelson Inc., publishers.

2) The Amplified Bible Copyright © 1965, 1987 by the Zondervan Corporation The Amplified New testament copyright © 1958, 1987 by the Lockman Foundation.

All materials used by permission

Loosing The Key of David: Minister's Guide
Copyright ©2009 by Stephen Fredericks
All Rights Reserved
Printed in the United States of America
Key of David Healing Ministries LLC., Kennesaw GA 30156

Dedicated to all of those who came before us
Making this ministry possible.
May the Lord bless and keep you ALL.

Table of Contents

	Introduction	i
1.	First Impressions	1
2.	Sins of the Fathers: Generational Sins	5
3.	In The Womb	7
4.	The Early Years (0-3)	11
5.	Performance Orientation / Procrastination	15
6.	Judging Parents & Others	19
7.	Inner Vows	23
8.	Forms of Replacement / Sibling Rivalry	25
9.	Bitter Roots: Judgments Create Expectations	29
10.	General Areas of Inner Healing &Deliverance	31
11.	Specific Areas of Inner Healing & Deliverance	35
12.	Deliverance, Casting Away Unclean Spirits	39
13.	Demerit Badges: Shame, Blame & Guilt	43
14.	How we See God / Forgiving Christians	45
15.	Soul ties, Formation & Severing	49
16.	Standing In Repentance	53
	Appendix A – A Sample Outline	A1
	Appendix B – The Homework	B1

Introduction

The Ministers Guide is intended for those seeking a quick refrence to the interview questions and prayers we offer in *Loosing The Key of David*. All of the interview questions and guided prayers offered in that volume are repeated here in a quick, easy to search easy to carry version. This 'pocket guide' is not a replacement for *Loosing The Key of David* as it does not discuss any of the topics. But if you are trying to identify an issue or set someone free in an area then this book can offers you a convenient solution.

The Session

While this guide is formatted to follow the general course of the ministry session, there are some notes that should be shared about the session itself. This ministry has no set format. This is a Holy Spirit led ministry and as such, can take many forms. I have ministered (using this discipline) at the altar, in street ministry, Sunday schools, conferences, one on one, and corporately. There is no hard fast rule for how it is to be done. The basic structure of the session does have some standard elements which are:

- The Interview
- Sharing
- Prayer

No matter the depth of ministry, these three remain.

The Interview

The basic interview includes asking many key questions that will help shed light on issues that need addressing. Time permitting, as much information as possible should be gained to allow for the most freedom. As you ask questions let the Holy Spirit guide you. As the questions are answered listen for the leading and guiding of the Holy Spirit. The Lord will give you insights as well as directing future questions.

Sharing

After the interview, share with the client what you have discerned through his/her answers and the promptings of the Holy Spirit, one subject at a time. Allow him/her the freedom to disagree with part or all of your assessment. If there is any agreement, move on to prayer. If there is none it is possible that he/she is not yet ready to receive or it is possible that you may have missed it. Even if you feel you have heard the voice of the Lord, you must concede that you are fallible or that the timing is not right. If there is no agreement, apologize to the client and let him/her go; letting he/she know you are there for him/her if they need you.

Prayer

If there is agreement, continue forward - leading him/her in prayers of confession, repentance and forgiveness. Some of the prayers you will lead them in, others you will pray over them.

The appendix section of this volume contains two additional resources ministers will find useful. The first is a sample outline complete with interview questions and sample prayers. This outline is meant to give the minister an idea of the direction a full session might take. The second is a copy of the homework we give each of our clients. This homework is designed to help the client keep the ground that was gained in his/her session. It is a set of good, life giving habits to replace the negative, self destructive habits he/she has just repented of and put to death on the cross.

Chapter 1 First Impression

Your relationship with Father God is founded on your relationship with your natural father.

Four Spiritual Laws: The foundational basis for this ministry

Just as God weaved natural laws into the universe (like gravity and inertia) to govern our natural existence, he has ordained spiritual laws to govern our spiritual existence. These laws are immutable and impersonal just like their natural counterparts. If you are convinced you can fly and jump off a roof, you are not going to defy gravity you are going to demonstrate it. Whether or not you believe in the law of gravity, it is a physical law. The spiritual laws that form the basis for this ministry are just as reliable.

1. The first commandment with a promise

"Honor your father and your mother, as the Lord your God commanded you, that your days may be prolonged and that it may go well with you in the land which the Lord your God gives you." (Deut 5:16)

2. The Law of Judgment

"Judge not, that you be not judged. For with what judgment you judge, you will be judged; and with the measure you use, it will be measured back to you." (Matt 7:1-2)

3. Laws of Sowing and Reaping & Increase

"Do not be deceived, God is not mocked; for whatever a man sows, that he will also reap." (Gal 6:7)

"[we] sow the wind and reap the whirlwind." (Hos 8:7)

4. Law of Forgiveness

Certainly one of the most difficult concepts on the earth is the concept of forgiveness. Peter struggled with this asking if he should forgive seven times. Jesus responded that he should forgive seventy times seven times. In fact in the Lords prayer he tells us to pray *"forgive us our trespasses (sins, debts, etc.) as we forgive those who trespass (sin, debts, etc.) against us."* Whatever the translation, "forgive us as we forgive" remains the same.

Forgiveness is so important that at the end of this prayer forgiveness is the one thing Jesus goes back to explain as soon as He finished praying. *"For if you forgive men their trespasses, your heavenly Father will also forgive you. But if you do not forgive men their trespasses, neither will your Father forgive your trespasses."* (Matt

6:14-15). If we want to be forgiven, forgiveness is not an option, it is a requirement.

This can be difficult because we may have a misguided view of what forgiveness is. Forgiveness is simply giving up your right to be angry with the one that has caused you hurt or offense. Forgiveness isn't saying that it's ok that someone hurt you. It is not saying that you are going to place yourself in a position to be hurt again. Forgiveness doesn't set the other person free - it sets us free!

To better understand forgiveness it is helpful to understand unforgiveness. When we choose not to forgive it is like drinking poison and waiting for the other person to die. Choosing not to forgive ultimately harms us. I have an example I like to use to illustrate this principle. Imagine you are driving down the freeway and someone cuts you off. You get really angry and even yell at them. Meanwhile they have continued driving down the road without giving you a second thought. Because you can't let it go, your anger festers and ruins your day, and they still haven't given you a second thought. Forgiveness in this instance becomes a lifeline, freeing us from the control of the other person.

First Impressions

Chapter 2 Generational Sins / Curses

The Interview:

- What diseases / illnesses that seem to filter down either mothers or fathers side of the family?
- Was money an issue when your mother / father were growing up?
- Was anyone in your family involved in the occult?
- Was anyone in your family involved in the Masons?
- Does violence run in either side of the family?
- Does addiction run in either side of the family?
- Has anyone in the family history turned from God?
- What nationality are you?

Guided Prayer:

Client Repeats: "Father, as Daniel repented for all of Israel, so I repent for all of my ancestors as far back as Adam who may have brought a curse on my bloodline. Father I repent for every ancestor who may have cursed your holy name. I repent for every ancestor who cursed Abraham. I repent for every ancestor who cursed your people Israel. Father I repent for every ancestor who cursed your plan for their life.

Heavenly Father I reverse every curse because I choose to bless your holy name, I bless father Abraham, I bless your people Israel. Father I embrace your plan for my life and that of my family in Jesus Holy Name."

As you have repented for your ancestors as far back as Adam the Lord is severing every generational curse of (list specifics from interview). The Lord is severing from off mother's side and father's side as far back as Adam every generational curse. The Lord is loosing his angels to war in the Heavenlies on your behalf. He is loosing the key of David with which he shuts and no one opens and he is shutting every door the enemy has used to gain access to you through your ancestors sin.

Client Repeats: "Heavenly Father I call forth every anointing, every calling, and every blessing, physical, emotional, spiritual, and even financial blessing that my ancestors refused to pick up, left lying in the dirt, Father I call them forth into my bosom. Father I call forth my birthright in Jesus holy name."

The Lord is going back as far as Adam. He is gathering every calling, anointing, and blessing, physical, emotional, spiritual and even financial blessings, that your ancestors have left and he is placing them in you.

He is granting you your birthright in Jesus holy name.

Chapter 3 In-Utero Wounds

The Interview:

- How many brothers and sisters were you raised with?
- What is the eldest's name and how many years older are they than you?
- Where were you in the birthing order?
- Any miscarriages before you were born?
- Do you know what kind of pregnancy your mother had with you? Were you early, late, or any complications?
- Do you ever feel as though you don't fit in anywhere?
- Do you feel as though there is greatness inside of you that can't get out?
- Do you find that you often sabotage yourself?
- Have you ever felt as though you didn't belong or fit in anywhere?
- Did you have a problem with stealing, or lying as a child, or even as an adult?

Guided Prayer:

The Lord is going to your conception. He is the Alpha and Omega, the beginning and the end. Time and space can't hinder Him. He is omnipresent. He is at your conception and is holding in His left hand the egg and in His right hand the seed ... cleansing the egg and the seed from all defilement, fear, ambivalence, confusion, (specifics from interview) (immorality if conceived out of wedlock). As He puts

His hands together, He is creating this wonderful union which is (client's name). He is breathing life into you and you into your mother's womb.

Client Repeats: "I repent for my spiritual rebellion and for opening any door that would give Satan an opportunity to gain entrance into me. I put my death wish and spiritual rebellion to death on the cross. I choose life and I choose blessings."

The Lord is reaching into the depths of your soul and spinning your spirit within your chest, turning it forward until it is in direct alignment with your soul and body, so that you will receive directly from Father God all that He has purposed for you to receive, feel, and accomplish. I call your slumbering spirit to awaken in Jesus' name.

Mother's ambivalence:
- Everything your mother ate, and drank affected your body.
- Every profound thought and feeling affected your spirit.
- "I hope it's a girl! .... but money is tight."
- "I'm so excited! ... But will it hurt?"
- Ambivalence lays like a cloak across your spirit creating those ups & downs in your life It hinders you from continuing in a positive direction you get close to success & fall backward

God is flooding your mother's womb with His blood ... cleansing it from all defilement and death. Heavenly Father, send your Holy Spirit to wash all ambivalence off (client's) spirit with the Blood of Jesus ... so their spirit can take hold of life as Jesus intended. (If orphan spirit is present) God is lifting up your orphan spirit that always feels like it doesn't fit in... where you always feel like you are on the outside looking in. He is nurturing you and holding you close ... saying this is your space, this is your place. I ask the Lord to heal the trauma of your birth

If conceived out of wedlock:

Client Repeats: "As an act of my will and by the authority of Jesus Christ, I cast far from me the bastard spirit. I cast this spirit into outer darkness. Heavenly Father, send your Holy Spirit and fill the void that this evil spirit has left. Fill me to overflowing with your peace, joy, life, and light."

Now I come into agreement with you...and cast the bastard spirit into outer darkness, Come Holy Spirit to fill every void with your life and light in Jesus' Holy name.

Client Repeats: "I forgive all those who might have spoken word curses over me while I was in my mother's womb. I set them all free. I repent for buying the lie. I choose to receive the word of the Lord that I am fearfully and wonderfully made. I was called by my first name, before the foundation of the world, by my Father God according to His purpose and glory. I choose life, I choose life, I choose life, and I choose blessings in Jesus' holy name!"

God is taking His sword and severing the umbilical chord between you and your mother He is clearing it of every hindrance and connecting it to Himself, so that His life can flow freely from Him through the umbilical chord into the depths of your soul filling you with hope, peace, confidence and courage.

Chapter 4: The Early Years; Our Earliest Reactions

The Interview:

- How many brothers and sisters were you raised with?
- Where were you in the birthing order?
- What is the eldest's name and how many years older are they than you?
- What kind of personalities did your brothers/sisters have i.e., angry, controlling, fearful, victims etc.?
- How do you get along with your children?
- Who did the discipline growing up? How would they handle it... with a switch, belt, or anything they could get their hands on?
- Would the other parent ever spank? How would they discipline?
- Did they ever lose control? Any unjust spankings?
- Were they ever abusive?
- Did you ever end up taking care of your baby sister/brother? Did you resent it? How old were you?
- Did you have any invisible friends as a child? Do you remember their names? (We are looking for familiar spirits)
- Any difficult or traumatic incidents in your childhood that trouble you now?
- Do you have any addictions?

Guided Prayer:

When you were crying in the night needing to be fed, nurtured or changed... the caretaker might have been angry, frustrated, fatigued ... and the caretaker's touch sent a message into the depths of your soul that said, "My need is not being met or if it gets met, I will have to pay a terrible price." These messages formed a void in the bottom of the soul and you have been trying to fill this void throughout your life with people, places, and things (specifics from interview), and nothing has satisfied. And no matter how happy you have ever been, you can hear that echo saying it will never last for you. As I pray this prayer over you, the hand of God is going to seal this void, and He is going to pour in new wine, new oil, new milk, new bread, and the water of the Holy Spirit. And for the first time in your life, you're going to experience the comfort, peace, and joy of Almighty God.

Earliest Reactions

(When you were crying in the night because of hunger, pain, discomfort. Your need got met, but the Caretaker's touch might have been, angry, frustrated, absent, or fatigued. The message to the spirit is, "My need will get met, but I don't deserve it, not without me suffering some consequence, not without me feeling pain, guilt, shame. I must not deserve to have my needs met.")

Lord, there is a little one deep inside (name of client) who is afraid, lonely, hurting, angry and hungry. They need to be held in arms, which are secure and strong. Thank you, Father, that your arms are like that, and that right now you are reaching deep down inside to enfold little baby name with the warmth and strength of your own being. I know that you, Father, are delighted with the little one whom you fashioned out of your own heart of love. This one, Lord, is chosen and precious, a treasure to you. You are pouring your sweet light into your child until all hunger is satisfied; all anxiety is settled out, all fears are calmed. Hold this one, Lord, until the love that you are permeates every cell of name being, and enables them to melt into you, trusting. Thank you Father, that you are light pushing back darkness, you are music displacing noise, you are a perfectly safe place to lie down and rest. You will never leave (client's name) nor will your love fail them.

Client Repeats: "Father, I take the responsibility for the choices that I have made, I confess attitudes which planted the original problems in my life, and I lay the entire matter on the altar of God, giving myself to You Lord without explanation or defense.

Father I thank you for bringing to death the old structure with its practices. Comfort and strengthen me from the inside, give me a new heart, and grow me up into the fullness of my new life in Jesus holy name. Amen"

Lord Jesus, go back into (client's name) life when the foundation of basic trust should have been formed, but wasn't. We ask you to comfort and nurture your child. Show them how much you cherish them. Build in them what has never been there... trust. Allow your blood to seal every breach, every break, and every chip. Let your love and solidity build that basic trust.

Client Repeats: "Father, I confess I do not trust. This lack of trust has hindered my walk with you and permeated my life. I know I must trust, but I cannot build it in myself. I forgive my parents for their lack of provision ... emotional, spiritual, physical, and financial. Now build in me that which was never there ... trust ... and restore the years that Satan has stolen, and I have squandered."

Earliest Reactions

Chapter 5: Structures of Performance Orientation / Procrastination

The Interview:

- Do you know what kind of pregnancy your mother had with you?
- What kind of personality did your dad have? How about your mom?
- Growing up, did you feel as though you couldn't please your mom/dad?
- How old were you when you accepted the Lord?
- If you died today, where would you be?
- If Jesus stood at the gate, and asked "Why should I let you into my Heaven?" What would your answer be?
- If you read the Word a little more, would God be more pleased with you?
- Is there anything that you know God has forgiven you for, but are finding it hard to forgive yourself?
- Have you ever had a hard time meeting deadlines?
- When Mom / Dad came home were they 'home' or did other things occupy their time?
- Have you ever struggled with tardiness? / Were you early for everything?
- Did you eat as a family growing up? At the table? What kind of conversation would take place?
- How would you spend time with your mom / dad growing up?

Guided Prayer:

Client Repeats: "We have judged our mother & father that we couldn't trust them. We judged that they betrayed us, stole from us, and lied to us.

(An unspoken promise made at conception: that the child is loved, wanted, and made secure & safe. When it doesn't happen, the child is lied to and stolen from.)

Performance Orientation:

Client Repeats: "We took upon ourselves a structure called Performance Orientation where we have had to earn our right to live, earn our right to exist, earn everyone's love, acceptance, and appreciation ... including Yours Lord. But we knew we were never going to be good enough, smart enough, worthy enough, lovable enough, deserving enough. We pick up the Word of God like a sledgehammer and shatter the structure of Performance Orientation and we pick up the pieces and put them to death on the cross. We want to finally rest in the blessed assurance that Your love for us is truly unconditional ... not based on what we do, how good we are, how holy we are, but based simply on the fact that you can't help Yourself Lord. You have got to love us because you called us, chose us, and knew us before the foundation of the world. You knew what we were going to think, say, or do before we ever thought, said it, or did it and You love us anyway ... and we can rest in that."

Procrastination:

Client Repeats: "Father, we have judged our mother and father that we were never a priority in their life. Not in any boy or girl's life, man or woman, our children, our spouse (say their name), no authority's life, no society's life ... not even in your life Lord. And since we are not a priority, we cannot establish priorities, order priorities, or meet priorities. We use procrastination as a weapon to prove how unworthy we are. And if someone tries to make us a priority, we must prove to them, to God, and to ourselves how unworthy we really are. We must sabotage every relationship and self-destruct to prove how unworthy we truly are. We repent of this, Lord."

Driven:

Client Repeats: "Father, we have judged our mother and father that we were never a priority in their life. Not in any boy or girl's life, man or woman, our children, our spouse (say their name), no authority's life, no society's life ... not even in your life Lord. And since we are not a priority, we cannot establish priorities, order priorities, or meet priorities. We take on more than we can handle to prove how unworthy and incapable we are. And if someone tries to make us a priority, we must prove to them, to God, and to ourselves how unworthy we really are. We must sabotage every relationship and self-destruct to prove how unworthy we truly are. We repent of this, Lord."

Performance Orientation

Prayer for the structures above:

As you have confessed and repented for these structures, shattering them and putting the pieces to death on his cross I speak the forgiveness of Almighty God over you.

Lord, just as Elijah called down the fire to consume the sacrifice, so I call down your holy fire to consume this structure. Father I pray that nothing remains of it for client to try to rebuild. Father I thank you that your love is sufficient and there is nothing we can do to earn it. Nor is there anything we can do to lose it but Father your love is truly unconditional and we can rest in that. In Jesus name Amen.

Chapter 6: Judging Your Parents

The Interview:

- What kind of personalities did your brothers/sisters have i.e., angry, controlling, fearful, victims etc.
- Are your brothers and sisters married? If so, married more than once? (If yes) What broke up the first marriage? Other marriages... How is their current marriage? Are they happy? (Ask these questions for each sibling)
- Have you been married more than once? If so, what broke it up?
- If you could change one thing about your spouse, what would it be? What's the one thing your spouse would change about you?
- How do you get along with your children?
- Do you know what kind of pregnancy your mother had with you? Were you early, late, or any complications?
- What kind of work did your dad do while you were growing up?
- What kind of personality did your dad have? How about your mom?
- Were they ever abusive?
- Would mom and dad fight a lot? What would they fight about? Tell me how old you were, and then tell me what happened, and how you reacted.
- Growing up, did you feel as though you couldn't please your mom/dad?

- Who did the discipline?
- How would they handle it... with a switch, belt, or anything they could get their hands on?
- Did they ever lose control? Any unjust spankings?
- Would the other parent ever spank? How would they discipline?
- Did you ever end up taking care of your baby sister/brother? Did you resent it? How old were you?
- Any difficult or traumatic incidents in your childhood that trouble you now?
- Have you had any affairs? With a married person?
- Do you struggle with procrastination (putting off to the last minute those things that need to be done)?
- Did you have a problem with stealing, or lying as a child, or even as an adult?

Guided Prayer:

(Because the specific judgments vary in every case there is no specific prayer to pray. All judgments must be confessed repented of and forgiven)

Client Repeats: "Heavenly Father I confess I judged my mother to be, specifics from interview. Father I repent for judging her and I ask you to forgive me. Please come and reap all that I have sown."

As you have confessed and repented for judging your mother I speak the forgiveness of Almighty God over you. Lord we ask you to reap all that has been sown and to lift client out of this field of weeds and thorns and to place them in a field they did not sow, to reap a harvest they did not plant. Lift them out of darkness and into your glorious light.

Client Repeats: "Heavenly Father I confess I judged my father to be, specifics from interview. Lord I repent for judging him and I ask you to forgive me. Please come and reap all that I have sown."

As you have confessed and repented for judging your father I speak the forgiveness of Almighty God over you. Lord we ask you to reap all that has been sown and to lift client out of this field of weeds and thorns and to place them in a field they did not sow, to reap a harvest they did not plant. Lift them out of darkness and into your glorious light.

Client Repeats: "Father God, we choose to forgive our mother and father, siblings, every boy & girl, (my own children), every man & woman, my spouse, all authority, all society ... We even forgive You, Lord for putting us in this family. We forgive ourselves. Come Lord Jesus and reap all that we have sown. Give us a glorious opposite."

Judging Parents is so integral in the Inner Healing process that no one prayer can hope to cover all of the ramifications. It is interwoven in every other area of this process and as such will be prayed throughout.

Chapter 7: Inner Vows

The Interview:

(Because most inner vows remain hidden it is necessary to gauge them by the fruit in the client's life.)
- Do you find it easier to pray for someone than to have someone pray for you?
- Do you feel the need to pray for someone who has just prayed for you?
- Do you ever feel isolated, alone?
- Do you find that people have a hard time relating to / understanding you?
- Do you remember any times in childhood when you said, "I'll never / always … when I grow up?"
- Do you reject people before they reject you?

Guided Prayer:

Heavenly Father, lift your child out of this stronghold they've built. What they meant to protect them has become a prison keeping them from entering into relationships with family, friends, and even with you Lord. Father now send your Holy Spirit like a flood to erode the foundations of these walls. Let your love, grace, mercy, and healing topple the walls of this fortress so that not one stone stands on another. Now Father, be for them a strong tower; for you are a strong tower that the righteous run into and are safe. You have called client righteous. Father replace this heart of stone with the heart of your son our Lord Jesus. Let their heart beat in time with his own.

Chapter 8: Forms of Replacement & Sibling Rivalry

The Interview:

- How many brothers and sisters were you raised with?
- What is the eldest's name and how many years older are they than you?
- Where were you in the birthing order?
- Any miscarriages before you were born?
- What kind of personalities did your brothers/sisters have i.e., angry, controlling, fearful, victims etc.
- Are your brothers and sisters married? If so, married more than once? (If yes) What broke up the first marriage? Other marriages... How is their current marriage? Are they happy? (Ask these questions for each sibling)
- How did you get along with your brothers / sisters?
- What kind of pregnancy your mother had with you? Were you early, late, or any complications?
- Did you ever end up taking care of your baby sister/brother? Did you resent it? How old were you?
- Were both parents present when you were growing up?
- Did anyone ever touch you inappropriately, if so, how old were you, and by who?
- Did you tell? How long did that go on?

Replacement & Rivalry

Guided Prayer

(Confess judgments/resentment for replacing/being replaced by brother/sister.)

Client Repeats: "Lord I have taken upon myself the structure of Parental Inversion, I repent for taking your job, and I pick up the Word of God like a sledge hammer, and I shatter the structure of parental inversion and put the pieces to death on the cross. Now I give you back your job Lord in Jesus name. Amen."

You have taken His word like a sledgehammer and shattered this structure, placing the pieces on His cross. Now Lord I ask you to consume this offering with your holy fire that client couldn't rebuild it even if they wanted to.

Client Repeats: "Lord I have taken upon myself the structure of Substitute Mate, I repent for taking (mother's / father's) place, emotionally, spiritually, physically, and I pick up the Word of God like a sledge hammer, and I shatter the structure of substitute mate and put the pieces to death on the cross in Jesus name. Amen."

You have taken His word like a sledgehammer and shattered this structure, placing the pieces on His cross. Now Lord I ask you to consume this offering with your holy fire that client couldn't rebuild it even if they wanted to.

Replacement & Rivalry

Client Repeats: "Father God, we choose to forgive our mother and father, siblings, every boy & girl, (my own children), every man & woman, my spouse, all authority, all society ... We even forgive You, Lord for putting us in this family. We forgive ourselves. Come Lord Jesus and reap all that we have sown."

Replacement & Rivalry

Chapter 9: Bitter Roots: Judgments Creating Expectations

The Interview:

(Any of the questions from Chapter 6 can reveal Bitter Root Judgments & Expectations)

- Have you been married more than once? If so, what broke it up?
- If you could change one thing about your spouse, what would it be? What's the one thing your spouse would change about you?
- How do you get along with your children?
- What kind of personality did your dad have? How about your mom?

Guided Prayer:

Now the Lord Jesus Christ is taking His severe sword, going down into your soul of souls and severing every bitter root judgment, severing every bitter root expectation. He is going back as far as your infancy and healing every trauma that you have ever suffered, emotional, spiritual, physical, and even sexual. He is pulling out of the Heavenlies every word curse spoken over you by anyone, including those word curses you have spoken over yourself ... and throwing them at the foot of His cross. He is severing every restriction that has kept you from walking in His freedom or the fullness of His life. He is crushing every signaling device and antenna that has been raised listening for the offense.

God is erasing every lie whispered into your ear, spirit, mind, and soul and replacing them with truth." "You are fearfully and wonderfully made" "Greater is He that is in you than He that is in the world." "My God shall supply all of your needs according to His riches in Glory by Christ Jesus" (any other Scriptures that God lays on your heart)

Client Repeats: "I put to death on the cross every habit, pattern, and structure that has hindered my walk with You Lord, i.e. anger, rage, inability to trust, fear, negative outlook, procrastination, fornication, pornography, etc. (specifics from interview). Now give me a glorious opposite in Jesus' name."

The Lord is erecting a new signaling device and a new antenna. This new signaling device is sending out the signal that you are worth taking the time to get to know. You are loved, accepted and worthy of their time, attention, and affirmation / affection. This new antenna is listening for the first syllable of the first word of need. Now that you have been set free He is positioning you to help others. The focus is off of how you have been or will be treated and is now on how you can be used by him to heal and help his other children. Freely you have received now freely give in Jesus holy name. Amen.

Chapter 10: The Common Struggle; Prayers of Deliverance (Common)

The Interview:

Slumbering Spirit:
- Do you find yourself standing in worship wondering why everyone around you is receiving but not you?
- Do you take a long time to recover from illnesses?
- Do you have a hard time entering into the things of God?

Captive Spirit:
- Do you feel there is greatness in you that can't seem to bust out?
- Do you feel like there is a better version of you in there somewhere?
- Do you have any phobias, or deep rooted fears (dark, close spaces, snakes, heights, etc)?

Depression:
- Do you struggle with depression?
- Does it feel like it will never get better? (discerning between depression & Despondency)

Guided Prayer:

Slumbering Spirit:

Client Repeats: "Lord, I recognize my spirit is not fully functional, not fully awake in several areas. For some reason (*confess if known*) my spirit chose not to enter into life. I confess this as sin; I have put my light under a bushel. Like Jonah, I have fled from the life you designed for me. And, as with Jonah, my refusal to live in these areas has caused trouble. I ask your forgiveness for the ways I have wounded those around me Lord. I ask your forgiveness for being unwilling to live life."

As you have confessed and repented for not engaging in life I speak the forgiveness of Almighty God over you. I say you are forgiven. The Lord is washing your sin into the Sea of Forgetfulness where He remembers it no more.

Client Repeats: "Father I ask you to awaken my spirit. Cleanse my spirit and remove the cobwebs. I choose life. I choose to be present and I choose to engage. Bring to death Lord that impulse to hide and to flee. Help me to see your call to life as a loving call. Help me to see the call of those who love me in the same way. Open my ears Lord that I might hear your call and the call of my loved ones. In Jesus Name."

Lord I thank you for opening (client's name) ears so they may hear your call to life. I thank you that you are giving them courage to stand in adversity. (Client's name) I call your slumbering spirit to awaken in Jesus Holy Name.

Captive Spirit:

Client Repeats: "Father I am not complete. The enemy has stolen that which is mine. He has taken my spirit captive and has left me bound in fear (*specific from interview*). Father I ask you to free my spirit and return it to me. Take back what the enemy has stolen and restore the years. Make me whole in Jesus Holy name."

The Lord is not hindered by time or space. Right now he is going to that prison (*use specific fears from interview*) and he is unlocking your prison door. He is taking you by the hand and he is leading you out of darkness into His glorious light. The Lord is knitting your spirit together with your soul and body and He is making you every whit whole in Jesus holy name.

Depression:

Father I ask you to come into the darkness that is (Client's name) life right now. All energies, spiritual, emotional, and physical are used up. Lord they have called out to You and heard no answer. Nothing changed.

I ask you Lord to come and rekindle the flame of (Client's name) spirit. Little by little, and at a pace they can bear. Increase your light and energize their spirit. Jesus come and let the warmth of Your presence flow from the center of his being outward. He may not feel any immediate difference. That's okay. I know, Lord, in time, the good feelings will come.

Father I ask that you bless (Client's name) sleep so that rest reaches deep into the exhaustion. Begin the renewal process in Jesus Holy Name.

(There is no prayer of repentance for depression. The client truly suffering from this is not in a place to repent. Healing is required before the client can turn the eye inward to find those areas where repentance is needed.)

Chapter 11: Prayers of Deliverance (Uncommon)

The Interview:

Burden Bearing

- Do you feel like you need to help others?
- Do you find yourself empathizing with their pain?
- Do friends, family, etc. often unload their troubles on you?
- Do you feel like there is no one else who can / will help so you must?

Occult Involvement

- Have you ever been involved in the occult?
- Have you ever been to a psychic?
- Have you ever played with a Ouija board, tarot cards, rune stones or the like?
- Did you have any invisible playmates as a child?
- Where you or any member of your family part of the Masons, or Eastern Star?
- Where you or any member of your family part of Wicca, druids, or in any way involved in witchcraft?
- Have you been part of 'fringe Christian' groups like Latter Day Saints or Jehovah's Witness?

Physical Disease

(These should be ascertained when making the appointment preferably so adequate preparation can be made.)

- What diseases run through your family lineage?
- Are you feeling any pains in your body right now?
- What diseases have you been diagnosed with?

Guided Prayer

Burden Bearing

Client Repeats: "Heavenly Father you gave me this gift of Burden Bearing. But this gift has become a curse. I confess I have carried everyone's burdens. I have carried them in my flesh and in my emotions and they have overwhelmed me. I repent for misusing this gift and for not trusting in you. Father I take all of these burdens and I hurl them to the foot of your cross along with the yoke of burden bearing. Father, teach me how to use this gift for your glory in Jesus Holy name."

As you have confessed and repented for carrying burdens that were not yours and for carrying them wrongly, in your flesh and your emotions, I speak the forgiveness of Almighty God over you. He is washing these burdens from you and cleansing you from all defilement. He is breaking the yoke of burden bearing from off of your shoulders. You will now only carry the burdens He gives you. You will carry them only in the spirit and only as far as his cross as He intended. For His burden is light and His yoke is easy.

Father I thank you that you are taking this gift from (Client's name) and you are redefining it. Father you are giving it back to them with understanding that they need *only* carry the burdens you give them and then *only* as far as your cross. Father they are not to let these burdens get into their emotions or effect their flesh but they will carry them *only* in their spirits as you intend in Jesus holy name."

Occult Involvement

Client Repeats: "Father your word forbids us from seeking after the occult. I confess and repent that I have done that which is forbidden (Have client repent for specifics from interview). I repent for any participation I have had with the occult, Baal worship, witchcraft and spiritual assignments. I thank you Lord for breaking them off of me and off of my bloodline. Lord please reap all that I have sown."

God is severing off your bloodline every disease, every sin, every curse, and every form of addiction, every form of witchcraft, or spiritual assignment in Jesus Holy Name.

Deliverance Uncommon

The Lord is taking His severe sword (from Isaiah 27:1) and is severing the bonds that you made with: (list the things they bonded with).

Any bonding with: Baal Worship (mixing sexual perversion with worship)

Poverty	Familiar spirits
Infirmity	Jealousy
Addictions	Voodoo
Pornography	Witchcraft
Envy	homosexuality
Etc.	

Client Repeats: "Father, I repent for bonding with any of these curses, sins, addictions or spiritual assignments. I thank you Lord for my deliverance."

Physical Disease

(Because the spiritual roots of diseases are wide and varied I suggest researching them in "A More Excellent Way" By Pastor Henry Wright. Lead the client in repentance and forgiveness in the areas necessary and speak forgiveness and healing over them in the name of Jesus.)

Chapter 12: Deliverance, The Casting Away of Unclean Spirits.

The Interview:

The unclean spirits at work in the client's life will be revealed throughout the interview process. Pay special attention to these questions but let the Holy Spirit lead you throughout the interview.

- What brings you to see me today?
- If you could change one thing about your spouse, what would it be? What's the one thing your spouse would change about you?
- How do you get along with your children?
- Do you ever feel as though you don't fit in anywhere? (Orphan Spirit)
- Do you feel as though there is greatness inside of you that can't get out? (captive spirit)
- Do you find that you often sabotage yourself?
- What kind of personality did your dad have? How about your mom?
- Did you have any invisible friends as a child? Do you remember their names? (familiar spirits)
- Any difficult or traumatic incidents in your childhood that trouble you now?
- Is there anything that you know God has forgiven you for, but are finding it hard to forgive yourself? (Shame, Blame Guilt)

Guided Prayer:

Review interview sheet and have client cast evil spirits into outer darkness. (Let the Holy Spirit lead):

Client Repeats: "As an act of my will and by the authority of Jesus Christ I cast far from me the spirit of (list & repeat) never to return. Heavenly Father, send your Holy Spirit and fill the void where these evil spirits have left. Fill me to overflowing with your peace, joy, life, and light.

Spirits of:

Despair	division	unforgiveness
Rejection	loneliness	separation
Jealousy	lying spirit	isolation
Detachment	envy	deception
Intimidation	confusion	pride
Lust	religious	confounding
Rebellion	anger	rage
Fear	inadequacy	sabotage
Self-abuse	depression	incompletion
Deaf & dumb	abandonment	inconsolable
Sadness	Molech	low self-esteem
Low self-worth	invalidation	invisibility
Incubus/Succubus		Sexually Perverse

Unclean Spirits

Now I come into agreement with you... casting these evil spirits far from you *never* to return. Heavenly Father, send your Holy spirit to fill every void that every evil spirit has left with Your life and light.

The Holy Spirit is rising within you like a fountain of living water rising up out of your belly. As it rises within you it is enveloping your heart, eroding and washing away your walls of stone. The Holy Spirit is replacing your heart of stone with the heart of our Lord and Savior Jesus. He is causing your heart to beat in time with his own so when you place your hand on your chest it is no longer your heartbeat you are feeling but his. As he continues rising within you he is cleansing your mind. He is scouring the three levels of your mind; the conscious, subconscious, even unconscious. He is renewing your mind; giving you the mind of Christ.

Now just as a glass filled to overflowing so the water of the Holy Spirit is spilling out of the crown of your head and flowing down, covering your ears, so that he is washing the blockages from your ears. Every word spoken to you will now be filtered by the Holy Spirit and you will no longer hear the word but the spirit by which the word was spoken. You will hear the Lord more clearly than ever before. As the Holy Spirit flows over your eyes He is washing the scales from your eyes. You will no longer see people after the flesh but according to the Spirit. The Lord is opening your spiritual eyes to see. He continues pouring down over your lips and every word you speak will be filtered by the Holy Spirit. Others will no longer misunderstand your words because they are filtered by Almighty God.

As he flows down over your shoulders he is washing away every burden you have carried wrongly in your flesh or emotions. He is washing these burdens to the foot of his cross. And as He covers your arms He is giving you the strength to carry the burdens he gives you, but only in your spirit and only as far as His cross as He intended. As He flows over your hands, He is placing healing in your hands. Everything you set your hand to do will prosper because he has touched it first.

As he continues to flow down he is covering your legs, giving you the strength to stand in adversity. As he washes over your feet he is preparing you to walk in peace. Everywhere you set your foot is holy ground for He has stepped there first. And just as water pools around the base of the glass so too the Holy Spirit is spreading out from around you so that anyone who gets within three feet of you can't help but feel His presence.

People will no longer see the spirit that is in you. Rather they will see you in the Holy Spirit in Jesus holy name. Amen.

Chapter 13: Demerit Badges, Shame Blame & Guilt

The Interview

- Is there anything you feel God has forgiven you for that you're having a hard time forgiving yourself for?
- Are there any traumatic incidents from childhood that still bother you?
- Is there anything we haven't talked about, understanding that if you leave it in the dark Satan can still use it against you, anything you bring into the light God is ready and willing to release you from?

(Shame Blame & Guilt come through many of the actions and judgments made in childhood, be listening for signs of their presence throughout the interview as well)

Guided Prayer

Client Repeats: "You say in Your Word Lord that if we repent, You are faithful and just to forgive. And I receive your forgiveness. But to show You how sincere I am and how serious these sins were, I'm going to hang on to a little bit of the shame, blame, guilt, and regret just to show You how much I love you."

You may not have said these words, but you told me you could not forgive yourself or still had regret for past sins. When you do this, Satan falls over laughing and God sees this in a totally different way. God says, **client**, why would you pull my son's beard out of His face once again? ...jam the crown of thorns on His head once again? ... Lay His back open and drive the nails through His wrists and feet? Why would you say that My Son's horrid death on the cross for you wasn't good enough? Not just to wash away your sin, but also the shame, blame, guilt, and regret associated with those sins.

Client Repeats: "Lord, you say in Your Word (in Hosea 4:6) that My people are destroyed for a lack of knowledge. Well, now we have that knowledge. We lay every sin we have ever committed from the day of our birth to this very moment at the foot of your cross, along with its shame, blame, guilt, and regret.

Father, I ask forgiveness for every sin that I have ever committed." (Have the client confess all of the sins that they shared with you during the interview adultery, stealing lying, etc. If abortion was involved, make sure they pray, "Forgive me Lord for murdering my baby."

Chapter 14: How we see God / Forgiving Christians

The Interview:

- How old were you when you accepted the Lord?
- If you died today, where would you be?
- If Jesus stood at the gate, and asked "Why should I let you into my Heaven?" What would your answer be?
- If you read the Word a little more, would God be more pleased with you?
- Have you ever disappointed God?
- Have you ever been mad at God?
- Have you ever been involved in a church split?
- Do you know what your love language is?
- Were you ever touched inappropriately as a child?
- When did you first have sex? Was it consensual? With someone your own age?
- Did you become promiscuous when you got older?
- Have you ever left a church angry?
- Has anyone called into question your salvation?

Guided Prayer:

Client Repeats: "Heavenly Father I confess I have no idea who you are. I have judged you and have believed the lies taught to me by others who said they knew you. Lord I repent for my judgments and I put the lies to death on your cross. I ask you to forgive me and to reveal yourself to me in a whole new way."

As you have confessed and repented, I speak the forgiveness of Almighty God over you. The Lord is erasing every lie you have believed about him. He is replacing these lies with his truth. That he is a father who will never leave you nor forsake you. He is your defender and protector. He is a perfectly safe place to lie down and rest. He is your provider. He loves you not because of anything you have done but because he created you and he can't help himself.

Client Repeats: "Father I confess I don't know how to love. My identifications of love are **(specifics from interview i.e. sex, sacrificing self, degrading self, being used, neglected, hurt, abused, rejected, mate being unavailable, controlled by mate, and being manipulated)**. I repent and ask you Lord to redefine love for and in me. Help me Lord to love as you do, sacrificially and unconditionally."

Client Repeats: "I forgive all Christians who hurt me, and all the hypocrisy that I have seen in Christianity and ministry, including my parents, pastors, deacons, elders, etc. I forgive every Christian who has fed me misinformation concerning who and what God is, and I put to death on the cross my identification of who and what God is, as well my identification of what love is."

The Lord is washing away your old identifications of love and renewing your heart to receive the love of Almighty God, pure, holy, righteous, and unconditional love. Now the Lord is taking you to the resurrection side of the cross and you are seeing Father God in a whole new way. You see Him as a Father, who will never leave you nor forsake you, reject you, defile you, abandon you, or harm you. You see Him as a Father who will always be there for you, always love you, nurture you, and hear you. He has made you a number one priority in His life. Since He has made you a priority, you can be a priority, and if someone tries to make you a priority, you can allow them to. You are good enough, smart enough, worthy enough, and worthwhile enough. Not because of who you are, but because of whose you are.

You are standing before Almighty God as an empty vessel, because you put to death on His cross, your identification of whom and what He is, as well as what your identification of what love is.

Client Repeats: "Father, send your Holy Spirit to fill this empty vessel. Fill me with the wisdom, truth, knowledge, and character of Almighty God. I want to experience Your compassion, mercy, and grace. Now fill this empty vessel with the love of Almighty God ... pure, holy, and righteous love. Lord make me whole, so that I don't need anyone to fill an empty place in me. I put to death on your cross my need to be needed. Fill me with Your love to such overflowing that I can allow my (future) husband/wife to be free to be themselves. He/she no longer has to perform to fulfill my desires or be what I need him/her to be, but rather he/she can give what he/she has, and I can receive it. I am whole and I am free to be myself, not what everyone expects me to be."

Chapter 15: Soul Ties & Sexual Sins

The Interview:

- How old were you when you became sexually active?
- Was it consensual? With someone your own age?
- Did you become promiscuous?
- How many sexual partners have you had? (Ask for first names)
- Were you touched inappropriately as a child?
- Do you have any friends who you feel are closer than a brother / sister?
- Have you ever been hurt in the church?
- Have you ever been hurt / betrayed by a friend?
- Do you have any strong relationships with unbelievers?
- Have you been involved in the occult?
- Are you part of a ministry in the church?
- Do you operate in any spiritual gifts?

Guided Prayer:

Client Repeats: "Father you created sex for a husband and wife. I confess that I used it for my own satisfaction and pleasure. I repent Lord for using it wrongly. In doing so Lord I formed soul ties with (List names from interview). Father I ask you to sever every ungodly soul tie I have made. I freely give back what is theirs and I ask you Lord to take back what is mine. Restore me Lord and make me whole that I may give myself to my husband / wife (Or future husband / wife if not married)."

The Lord is taking his severe sword and he is severing every ungodly soul tie you have formed with these men / women. He is sending back to them what is theirs' voiding every claim they hold on you and shutting every door they have used to gain access to you. What he shuts no one may open."

Client Repeats: "Father I repent for my ungodly relationships. These relationships have been unhealthy and have drawn me away from you. Father I allowed my relationships to become idols that I placed before you and I humbly repent. Father, sever every ungodly soul tie I have formed with (Specifics from interview). I freely give back to them what is theirs and I ask you to restore to me that which is mine in Jesus holy name."

As you have repented for your idolatrous relationships the Lord is taking his severe sword and smashing these idols. He is severing every ungodly soul tie you have formed with (specifics from interview). The Lord is sending back to them what is theirs, cancelling every spiritual assignment, debt and claim that they hold over you.

Now Heavenly Father as (client) has freely sent back what is theirs I call to the north, south, east and west and I call (client's) spirit back in Jesus holy name. The Lord is knitting your mind together with your soul and your spirit and he is making you whole, complete, and able to give yourself completely to your husband / wife ("the one God has for you" if not married).

Client Repeats: "Heavenly Father I repent for my involvement in (sexual perversions). As an act of my will and by the authority of Jesus Christ I cast far from me (specifics from interview i.e. the Homosexual spirit, Sexual Perverse Spirits, Incubus, Succubus, etc) never to return. I ask you Lord now to cleanse my mind body soul and spirit from all defilement. Father, send your Holy Spirit to fill me to overflowing with your love, mercy, grace, kindness, forgiveness, life and light in Jesus holy name."

As you have repented the Lord is faithful and just to forgive. I speak the forgiveness of Almighty God over you. The Lord is driving these spirits from you never to return. He is loosing His key of David shutting every door the enemy has used to gain entrance into you and what he shuts no one may open. The Lord is renewing your mind and reforming your identity in Him. He is speaking assurance to your spirit that he did not form you wrong and that you *are exactly* who he has called you to be. He is removing all ungodly impulses and desires restoring you to the perfect plan he had for you from the foundation of the world.

Chapter 16: Standing in Repentance

The Interview:

- What kind of personalities did your brothers/sisters have i.e., angry, controlling, fearful, victims etc.
- Are your brothers and sisters married? If so, married more than once? (If yes) What broke up the first marriage? Other marriages... How is their current marriage? Are they happy? (Ask these questions for each sibling)
- Have you been married more than once? If so, what broke it up?
- If you could change one thing about your spouse, what would it be? What's the one thing your spouse would change about you?
- How do you get along with your children?
- Do you know what kind of pregnancy your mother had with you? Were you early, late, or any complications?
- What kind of work did your dad do while you were growing up?
- What kind of personality did your dad have? How about your mom?
- Were they ever abusive?
- Would mom and dad fight a lot? What would they fight about? Tell me how old you were, and then tell me what happened, and how you reacted.
- Growing up, did you feel as though you couldn't please your mom/dad?

Standing in Repentance

- Who did the discipline?
- How would they handle it... with a switch, belt, or anything they could get their hands on?
  - Did they ever lose control? Any unjust spankings?
  - Would the other parent ever spank? How would they discipline?
  - Did you ever end up taking care of your baby sister/brother? Did you resent it? How old were you?
- Any difficult or traumatic incidents in your childhood that trouble you now?
- Have you had any affairs? With a married person?
- Do you struggle with procrastination (putting off to the last minute those things that need to be done)?
- Did you have a problem with stealing, or lying as a child, or even as an adult?

Guided Prayer:

(Client's name) I come to you now and I repent for every Christian, leader, pastor, elder, deacon (specifics from interview), who hurt you in His name. I repent for giving you false information about who he is and what it is to be a Christian. I repent for not allowing you to grow in and use you gifts in the church (and for any others that the interview or Holy Spirit reveal) can you forgive me?

Client Repeats: (Ask "Can you say,) "I forgive you?"

(After the client forgives) As you have forgiven I now speak the forgiveness of Almighty God over you. The Lord is revealing himself to you and to your spirit filling you with His holy presence in Jesus holy name.

Now (client's name) I come as your spiritual mom and I confess I (specifics from interview) can you forgive me?" (If client says "I forgive you mom" skip 'have client repeat' below)

Standing in Repentance

Client Repeats: (Ask "Can you say,) "I forgive you mom?"

(After client forgives mom say) Now I speak a mothers blessing over you (client's name). I say that you... (Let Holy Spirit lead you)

Now I come to you as your spiritual dad and I confess I (specifics from interview) can you forgive me? (If client says "I forgive you dad" skip 'have client repeat' below)

Client Repeats: (Ask "Can you say,) "I forgive you dad?"

(After client forgives dad say) Now I speak a fathers blessing over you (client's name). I call your spirit to life and you into the fullness of your manhood / womanhood. I call forth and bestow upon you your birthright. I say that you are the head and not the tail, above only and not beneath. You are blessed in the city and in the country, in the basket and in the store. Blessed is the fruit of your body. Your enemies come before you one way they will flee before you seven.

The Lord prepares a table before you in the presence of your enemies. He anoints your head with oil and your cup runs over. You are smart enough, holy enough, lovable enough, and strong enough. You are accepted in the beloved. And any man / woman would be crazy not to want you on their arm. You are a son / daughter of the Most High God and I dedicate you to Him and His purposes this day. I say grow and be and do all that He has called you to be from the foundation of the World in Jesus holy name.

(If client showed any embarrassment about their nationality of origin) "I come to you and I repent for everyone who has put you down, made you feel inferior, or tried to put you in your place because of your race. God is no respecter of persons; he created all of us and loves all of us unconditionally and equally. Can you forgive me for my ignorance and cruelty?"

Client Repeats: (Ask "Can you say,) "I forgive you?"

(After client forgives say) Now (client) as you have forgiven so you too can be forgiven. I speak the forgiveness of almighty God over you I declare the blessings of almighty God over you, every physical, financial, emotional, and spiritual blessing over you and your household in Jesus holy name.

Appendix A: A Sample Outline

1. Why have you come to see us?
   - Fruit: Fear Lust
   - Anger Low self-esteem
   - Loneliness Procrastination
   - Don't seem to fit in No desire for sex
2. Tell my story: What brought me to seek healing & how God changed me.
   Jesus freed me from anger, verbal abuse, etc.
   "This is pain (fist), this is anger (hand over fist) ... And this is nothing (hand over hand) you shove it down. You have red lenses over your eyes. You don't even know that they are there . I'm telling you that the wall is white, and you say it's red.
   Everything that you hear, feel or think is filtered through angry little kids. "If you will confess, repent, & forgive what I ask you to, you will walk out of here changed."
3. Share the 4 basic Scriptures:
   Your Relationship with Father God is only as good as your relationship with your natural father!
   1) The first commandment with a promise (Deut 5:16, Eph 6:2-3) "Honor your father and mother that it go well with you and that you enjoy long life on the earth." We dishonor our parents through judgment. "Judge not that ye be judged. For in the same way you judge others, you will be judged, and the same measure you use will be measured unto you." (Matt 7:1-2)
      - When a boy judges his father, he becomes him.
      - When he judges his mother, he marries her.
      - When a little girl judges her mother she becomes her
      - When she judges her father she marries him
      - Wounded spirits seek out wounded spirits, to fulfill the judgments they made as children .
   3) We reap what we sow (Gal 6:7). But not just what we sow, according to Hosea 8:7, we "Sow the wind, and reap the whirlwind!" This is the law of increase.
   4) The most difficult I saved for last! This is the most important aspect of the deliverance program. It starts the healing process! Without it there is no healing; without it, you cannot receive forgiveness; without it, don't bother to pray, sacrifice, or worship!

It encompasses love, humility, and obedience. Matt 6:12 ("as I forgive.") Forgiveness. Mathew 6:14-15 If you don't give it, you can't get it!

"Forgiveness is giving up the right to be angry with someone who has hurt you. It is not saying that it is all right that they hurt you, nor is it saying that you must put yourself in a position to be hurt again. When you forgive, you are set free, not the other person."

4. Two Things God Cannot Do:
   (a) Override your will. Do you agree with that?
   (b) Forgive you in areas where you have not forgiven. Do you agree with that?

The "tie-dye" shirt. (Knots not covered by the blood are unregenerate or unbelieving areas of your heart.)

PRAY: "Lord, I put to death on the cross all of my experience, knowledge, and expertise. I ask you
Holy Spirit to flow through me like a conduit. Thank you for the miracle that is about to take
place in (client's) life. I give you all the praise and glory for what You are about to do!"
- "This is not about mommy & daddy-bashing ... it's about your sinful responses to their actions."

QUESTIONS:
How many brothers and sisters were you raised with?
What is the oldest's name and how many years older is he/she than you?
Where were you in the birthing order?
Any miscarriages before you were born?
What kind of personalities did your brothers/sisters have i.e., angry, controlling, fearful, victims etc.
Are your brothers and sisters married? If so, married more than once?
(If yes) What broke up the first marriage? Other marriages...
How is their current marriage? Is he/she happy? (Ask these questions for each sibling)
Have you been married more than once? If so, what broke it up?

If you could change one thing about your spouse, what would it be?
What's the one thing your spouse would change about you?
How do you get along with your children?
Do you know what kind of pregnancy your mother had with you?
Were you early, late, or any complications?
What kind of work did your dad do while you were growing up?
Do you ever feel as though you don't fit in anywhere? Do you feel as though there is greatness inside of you that can't get out? (captive spirit) Do you find that you often sabotage yourself?
What kind of personality did your dad have? How about your mom? Was he/she ever abusive?
Would mom and dad fight a lot? If Yes, continue. If no, skip next two questions..
Tell me how old you were, and then tell me what happened, and how you reacted.
What would they fight about?
Growing up, did you feel as though you couldn't please your mom/dad?
Who did the discipline?
How would they handle it... with a switch, belt, or anything they could get their hands on?
Would the other parent ever spank? How would they discipline?
Did they ever lose control? Any unjust spankings?
Did you ever play show and tell with body parts as a kid? How old were you, and how many times did you
play, and with who? Did you get caught?
When did it stop?
Did anyone else ever touch you inappropriately, if so, how old were you, and by who?
Did you tell? How long did that go on?
Did you ever end up taking care of your baby sister/brother? Did you resent it? How old were you?
Did you have any invisible friends as a child? Do you remember their names? (We are looking for familiar spirits)
How old were you when you became sexually active?
Was it consensual, with someone your age?
Did you become promiscuous, as you got older?
Have you been involved with the occult, if so how old were you? (Ouija Boards, Tarot Cards, Psychics, etc...)
How old were you when you accepted the Lord?
If you died today, where would you be?

Sample Outline

If Jesus stood at the gate, and asked "Why should I let you into my Heaven?" What would your answer be?

If you read the Word a little more, would God be more pleased with you?

Have you ever had an abortion (i.e. been pregnant)? How old were you?

Any difficult or traumatic incidents in your childhood that trouble you now?

Is there anything else that we haven't talked about? Anything you greatly regret? Whatever you leave in the dark, the devil will try to beat you up with, whatever you bring into the light, God is ready to wash it all away under His Blood.

Have you had any affairs? (with a married person?)

Is there anything that you know God has forgiven you for, but are finding it hard to forgive yourself?

Have you ever felt as though you didn't belong or fit in anywhere? (orphan spirit)

What kind of illnesses seem to filter through your family, going as far back as you can remember...

grandparents, great grandparents, etc.?

Cancer Heart trouble High blood pressure

Diabetes Alcoholism Masons

Addiction in any form witchcraft (i.e. Santeria, satan worship, new age etc.)

What nationality are you? (Look for any embarrassment concerning national origin. This would be spiritual rebellion. Ancestors may have cursed Father Abraham.)

Do you struggle with procrastination (putting off to the last minute those things that need to be done.)

(The judgment here is not being a priority in anyone's life. Therefore I cannot set priorities, establish them or complete them. The client uses procrastination as a weapon against him/herself to prove how unworthy he/she is.) Please note! The client may not have a problem with procrastination. They may be driven, The judgment might still be that they were not a priority. They are striving to be a priority and find themselves sabotaging every relationship, by pushing people away, before he/she is pushed away, rejecting those who try to make them a priority fulfilling that judgement. Look at the fruit in his/her relationships. Did they all end badly?

Did you have a problem with stealing, or lying as a child, or even as an adult? (If he/she did or does, it started in the womb. There is an

unspoken promise that if I conceived you, you were wanted and loved, and you will be made to feel safe and secure. When this did not happen the spirit in the womb felt that he/she had been lied to and stolen from. He/she may find themselves lying or even stealing.)
Have you had any sexual encounters with anyone of the same sex? How about with animals? (If yes get the ages when these things occurred)

Note: Listen for the leading of the Holy Spirit throughout the questioning period. He might have you ask questions that are not listed or omit questions that are not relevant. The questions above are the most commonly asked questions that Sharon and I ask, but this list is not all-inclusive. Seek the Holy Spirit as you ask the questions and listen to the response of the client to determine what other line of questioning might be appropriate.

PRAYING WITH CLIENT
(Lead client to repeat items in bold print; all others are spoken by PDM.)
A. Generational:
1. **"Father, I repent for all my ancestors as far back as Adam who may have cursed Father Abraham ...**
Or stolen from Father God, which may have brought a curse on my bloodline. Now I reverse every curse because I bless Father Abraham, the Jewish people, Israel, Jerusalem, and I bless you Lord. I receive all the blessings God spoke over those who bless Father Abraham ...emotional, spiritual, physical, and financial blessings."

"I repent for any participation I have had with generational, sins, iniquities, curses, diseases,addictions, baalworship, witchcraft and spiritual assignments." I thank you Lord for breaking them off my bloodline...

"God is severing off your bloodline every generational disease, every generational sin, every curse, and every form of addiction, every form of witchcraft, or spiritual assignment on both your mother's and father's side."

2. Any bonding with: Baal Worship (mixing sexual perversion with worship)

Poverty	Familiar spirits	Infirmity
Jealousy	Addictions	Voodoo
Pornography	Witchcraft	Envy
Homosexuality	etc.	

(**PDM prays**) "We go all the way back to Noah.... and the Lord is taking His severe sword from (Isaiah 27:1) and is severing the bonds that you made with: (list the things they bonded with).

(Client repeats) "Father, I repent for bonding with any generational curses, sins, addictions or spiritual assignments. I thank you Lord for my deliverance."

B. In the womb:

(**PDM PRAYS**) "The Lord is going to your conception. He is the Alpha and Omega, the beginning and the end. Time and space can't hinder Him. He is omnipresent. He is at your conception and is holding in His left hand the egg and in His right hand the seed ... cleansing the egg and the seed from all defilement, fear, ambivalence, confusion, (specifics from interview) (immorality if conceived out of wedlock). As He puts His hands together, He is creating this wonderful union which is (client's name). He is breathing life into you and you into your mother's womb."

- Use open hand (child's spirit) on top of closed fist (body) illustration.
- If you felt unwanted, your spirit turned back to be with God.
- This is spiritual rebellion ...death wish...opens door to satan...legal right to mess with you.

(client repeats) "I repent for my spiritual rebellion and for opening any door that would give satan an opportunity to gain entrance into me. I put my death wish and spiritual rebellion to death on the cross. I choose life and I choose blessings."

Ask permission to lay your hand on client's chest ... (If PDM is a male and client is female, your female cover
will lay her hand on female client's chest)

(**PDM prays**) "The Lord is reaching into the depths of your soul and spinning your spirit within your chest, turning it forward until it is in direct alignment with your soul and body, so that you will receive directly from Father God all that He has purposed for you to receive, feel, and accomplish. I call your slumbering spirit to awaken in Jesus' name."

Mother's ambivalence:
-- Everything your mother ate, and drank affected your body.
-- Every profound thought and feeling affected your spirit.
-- "I hope it's a girl! .... but money is tight."
-- "I'm so excited! ... but will it hurt?"
-- Ambivalence lays like a cloak across your spirit
--creating those ups & downs in your life
-- It hinders you from continuing in a positive direction
-- you get close to success & fall backward

(**PDM prays**) "God is flooding your mother's womb with His blood ... cleansing it from all defilement and death. I ask the Holy Spirit to wash all ambivalence off your spirit with the Blood of Jesus ... so
your spirit can take hold of life as Jesus intended."

Orphan Spirit: "God is lifting up your orphan spirit that always feels like it doesn't fit in... where you always feel like you are on the outside looking in. He is nurturing you and holding you close ... saying this is your space, this is your place. God is widening your mother's birth canal to heal any trauma from birth."(If a C-section was done) "I ask the Lord to heal the trauma of your birth"

- If conceived out of wedlock, have client cast "Bastard spirit" out. (If client is a child call it an "Illegitimate spirit")

(**client repeats**) "**As an act of my will ... I cast far from me the bastard spirit Never to return. Come Holy Spirit and fill the void that these evil spirits have left. Fill me to overflowing with Your peace, joy, life, and light.**"

(**PDM Prays**) "Now I come into agreement with you...and cast these evil spirits from you never to return, and invite the Holy Spirit to fill every void with His life and light in Jesus' Holy name.

-- Renounce word curses spoken over them while in womb:
-- That they were a mistake, came too soon, should have been a girl/boy, were a burden or intrusion in the parent's life.
-- Spoken by parents, family, doctors, nurses, technicians who might have spoken word curses over them.

(client repeats) "I forgive all those who might have spoken word curses over me while I was in my mother's womb. I set them all free. I receive the word of the Lord that I am fearfully and wonderfully made. I was called by my first name, before the foundation of the world, by my Father God according to His purpose and glory. I choose life, I choose life, I choose life, and I choose blessings in Jesus' holy name!"

(**PDM prays**) "God is taking His sword and severing the umbilical chord between you and your mother and connecting it to Himself, for He truly is the giver of life. He is blowing every obstacle and hindrance out of that umbilical chord so that His life can flow freely from Him through the umbilical chord into the depths of your soul filling you with hope, peace, confidence and courage."

C. After the womb:
Age 0 to 3:
(**PDM prays**) "When you were crying in the night needing to be fed, nurtured, or changed... the caretaker might have been angry, frustrated, fatigued ... and the caretaker's touch sent a message into the depths of your soul that said, "My need is not being met or if it gets met, I will have to pay a terrible price." These messages formed a void in the bottom of the soul and you have been trying to fill this void throughout your life with people, places, and things (food if client is obese), and nothing has satisfied. And no matter how happy you have ever been, you can hear that echo saying it will never last for you. As I pray this prayer over you, the hand of God is going to seal this void, and He is going to pour in a new wine, a new oil, a new milk, a new bread, and the water of the Holy Spirit. And for the first time in your life, you're going to experience the comfort, peace, and joy of Almighty God."

Pray "The Mother's prayer" (This mother's prayer covers the following: Could not be breastfed, or breast-feeding had to be stopped. Oral fixation i.e., smoking or habitual eating.)

Ages infant to 3 crying in the night because of hunger, pain, discomfort. Your need got met, but theCaretaker's touch might have been, angry, frustrated, absent, or fatigued. The message to the spirit is, my need will get met, but I don't deserve it, not without me suffering some consequence, not without me feeling pain, guilt, shame. I must not deserve to have my needs met.

(**PDM prays**) Lord, there is a little one deep inside name of person who is afraid, lonely, hurting, angry and hungry. He/She needs to be held in arms, which are secure and strong. Thank you, Father, that your arms are like that, and that right now you are reaching deep down inside to enfold little baby (client's name) with the warmth and strength of your own being. I know that you, Father, are delighted with the little one whom you fashioned out of your own heart of love. This one, Lord, is chosen and precious, a treasure to you. You are pouring your sweet light into your child until all hunger is satisfied; all anxiety is settled out, all fears are calmed. Hold this one, Lord, until the love that you are permeates every cell of name being, and enables him/her to melt into you, trusting. Thank you Father, that you are light pushing back darkness; you are music displacing noise; you are a perfectly safe place to lie down and rest. You will never leave;
name nor will your love fail him/her.
(If the person is old enough to understand, have him/her repeat the following prayer after you)

(client repeats) Father, I take the responsibility for the choices that I have made, I confess attitudes which planted the original problems in my life, and I lay the entire matter on the altar of God, giving myself to You Lord without explanation or defense. Father I thank you for bringing to death the old structure with its practices. Comfort and strengthen me from the inside, give me a new heart, and grow me up into the fullness of my new life. In Jesus' Holy Name. Amen

Build Basic Trust: Age 0 to 3 ... When basic trust is formed and yours wasn't."

(**PDM prays**) "Lord Jesus, go back into (client's) life when the foundation of basic trust should have been formed, but wasn't. We ask you to comfort and nurture your child. Show him/her how much you cherish them. Build in him/her what has never been there... trust. Allow your blood to seal every breach, every break, every chip. Let your love and solidity build that basic trust"

(**client repeats**) "Father, I confess I do not trust. This lack of trust has hindered my walk with you and permeated my life. I know I must trust, but I cannot build it in myself. I forgive my parents for their lack of provision ... emotional, spiritual, physical, and financial. Now build in me that which was never there ... trust ... and restore the years that satan has stolen, and I have squandered."

Performance Orientation:

(**client repeats**) "I have judged my mother & father that I couldn't trust them. I judged that they betrayed me, stole from me, and lied to me.

Explain being lied to and stolen from in the womb. An unspoken promise made at conception: that the child is loved, wanted, and made secure & safe. When it doesn't happen, the child is lied to and stolen from.

(**client repeats**) "We took upon ourselves a structure called Performance Orientation where we have had to earn our right to live, earn our right to exist, earn everyone's love, acceptance, and appreciation ... including Yours Lord. But we knew we were never going to be good enough, smart enough, worthy enough, lovable enough, deserving enough. We pick up the Word of God like a sledgehammer and shatter the structure of Performance Orientation and we pick up the pieces and put them to death on the cross. We want to finally rest in the blessed assurance that Your love for us is truly unconditional ... not based on what we do, how good we are, how holy we are, but based simply on the fact that you can't help Yourself Lord. You have got to love us because you called us, chose us, knew us before the foundation of the world. You knew what we were going to think, say, or do before we ever thought, said it, or did it and You love us anyway ... and we can rest in that."

Age 3 to now:
Confess judging parents:
(client repeats) "Father, we have judged our father to be (specifics from interview, i.e. unavailable, angry, abusive, alcoholic, etc.) and therefore judged all men, (if female and married] even my husband, all boys, all authority, all society to be that way. We have even judged You Lord."

(client repeats) "Lord, we judged our mother that she was (specifics from interview, i.e. angry, critical & judgmental, controlling, abusive, etc.) and therefore judged all women, (if applicable my wife), all girls, all authority, all society to be that way."

Procrastination:
(client repeats) "Father, we have judged our mother and father that we were never a priority in their life. Not in any boy or girl's life, man or woman, our children, our spouse (say their
name), no authority's life, no society's life ... not even in Your life Lord. And since we are not a priority, we cannot set priorities, establish priorities, or complete priorities. We use procrastination as a weapon to prove how unworthy we are. And if someone tries to make us a priority, we must prove to them, to God, and to ourselves how unworthy we really are. We must sabotage every relationship and self-destruct to prove how unworthy we truly are. We repent of this, Lord."

Have client Confess judgments/resentment for replacing/being replaced by brother/sister.

Have client Confess and repent from other judgments, inner vows, etc. from interview.

After going through all ages 0 - now ...
(client repeats) "Father God, we choose to forgive our mother and father, siblings, every boy & girl, (my own children), every man & woman, my spouse, all authority, all society ... We even forgive You, Lord for putting us in this family. We forgive ourselves. Come Lord Jesus and reap all that we have sown."

Sample Outline

D. Client Casts Evil Spirits far from them never to return:
Review interview sheet and have client cast evil spirits far from them never to return. (let Holy Spirit lead):
(client repeats) "I use my will ... and I cast far from me the spirit of (list & repeat)*.""Come Holy Spirit and fill the void where these evil spirits have left. Fill me to overflowing with Your peace, joy, life, and light. Knit my mind, spirit, and soul together and make me whole."

(**PDM prays**) "Now I come into agreement with you...and I cast these evil spirits far from you never to return. Come Holy spirit and fill every void that every evil spirit has left with Your life and light.

* Spirits of:

Despair	abandonment	lust	low
Self-esteem	loneliness	envy	pride
Lying spirit	isolation	detachment	fear
Deception	intimidation	confusion	jealousy
Unforgiveness	religious	confounding	rebellion
Incubus/Succubus	anger	rage	seperation
(perverse, spirits)	inadequacy	sabotage	self-abuse
Depression	incompletion	deaf & dumb	division
Inconsolable	sadness	Molech	rejection
Low self-worth	invalidation	invisibility	elitism

E. Severing the Bitter Roots:
Explanation:
- Bitter root judgment: Law of God causing us to reap what we have sown when we judge someone.
- Bitter root expectation: A habit of self-fulfilling prophecy by which we "push" people to fulfill our picture of the way things will go. Example: "I'll always be rejected."

- Restriction: A band that wraps around the spirit, mind, body, & soul that keeps you from walking in the fullness of God's freedom .
-Signaling device: Puts out a signal all around you 24/7 saying: " Go ahead.... use me, abuse me, and throw me away...everybody always does."

-Antenna: Waits for the first syllable of the first word of the first sentence of the rejection. When it comes, you day: "See... I told you so...it happens every time...I'll always be rejected."

(**PDM Prays**) "Now the Lord Jesus Christ is taking His severe sword, going down into your soul of souls and severing every bitter root judgment, severing every bitter root expectation. He is going back as far as your infancy and healing every trauma that you have ever suffered ... emotional, spiritual, physical, and even sexual. He is pulling out of the heavenlies every word curse spoken over you by anyone, including those word curses you have spoken over yourself and throwing them at the foot of His cross. He is severing every restriction that has kept you from walking in His freedom or the fullness of His life. He is crushing every signaling device and antenna that has been raised listening for the offense. "God is erasing every lie whispered into your ear, spirit, mind, and soul and replacing them with truth." "You are fearfully and wonderfully made" "Greater is He that is in you than He that is in the world." "My God shall supply all of your needs according to His riches in Glory by
Christ Jesus" (any other Scriptures that God lays on your heart)

(client repeats) "I put to death on the cross every habit, pattern, and structure that has hindered my walk with You Lord, i.e. anger, rage, inability to trust, fear, negative outlook, procrastination, fornication, pornography, etc. (specifics from interview). Now give me a glorious opposite in Jesus' name."

F. Specific Prayers of Deliverance:
Pray various selected prayers for captive spirit, depression, addictions, etc.

G. Closing Prayers:
(client repeats) "You say in Your Word Lord that if we repent, You are faithful and just to forgive. And I receive your forgiveness. But to show You how sincere I am and how serious these sins were, I'm going to hang on to a little bit of the shame, blame, guilt, and regret just to show You how much I love you.

(**PDM prays**) "You may not have said these words, but you told me you could not forgive yourself or still had regret for past sins." "When you do this, satan falls over laughing because God sees this in a different way. God says, (client), why would you pull my son's beard out of His face once again? ...jam the crown of thorns on His head once again? ... lay His back open and drive the nails through His wrists and feet? Why would you say that My Son's horrid death on the cross for you was not quite good enough. Not just to wash away your sin, but also the shame, blame, guilt, and regret associated with those sins."

(**client Repeats**) "**Lord, you say in Your Word in Hosea 4:6 that My people are destroyed for a lack of knowledge. Well, now we have that knowledge and we lay every sin we have ever committed from the day of our birth to this very moment at the foot of Your cross ... along with its shame, blame, guilt, and regret.**"

(**client repeats**) "**Father, I ask forgiveness for every sin that I have ever committed.**" (Have the client confess all of the sins that they shared with you during the interview adultery, stealing lying, etc. If abortion was involved, make sure they pray, "**Forgive me Lord for murdering my baby.**")

(**client repeats**) "**I forgive all Christians who hurt me, and all the hypocrisy that I have seen in Christianity and ministry, including my parents, pastors, deacons, elders, etc. I forgive every Christian who has fed me misinformation concerning who and what God is, and I put to death on the cross my identification of who and what God is, as well my identification of what love is.**" "**My identification of love is: (list specifics from interview, i.e. sex, sacrificing self, degrading self, being used, neglected, hurt, abused, rejected, mate being unavailable, controlled by mate, and being manipulated) and I put it to death on the cross.**"

(PDM prays) "Now we watch your blood, Lord wash away every sin, all shame, all blame, all guilt into the sea of forgetfulness. You see it no more Lord and we finally receive our full pardon"

"I speak the forgiveness of God over you and call you into the fullness of your manhood / womanhood. The Blood of Jesus is covering you and the infant is stepping into the one yearold, the two-year old into the three year-old etc., all the way up until you are standing at the foot of the cross."

"Now the Lord is taking you to the resurrection side of the cross and you are seeing Father God in a whole new way. You see Him as a Father, who will never leave you nor forsake you, reject you, defile you, abandon you, or harm you. You see Him as a Father who will always be there for you, always love you, nurture you, and hear you. He has made you a number one priority in His life. Since He has made you a priority, you can be a priority, and if someone tries to make you a priority, you can allow them to. You are good enough, smart enough, worthy enough, and worthwhile enough. Not because of who you are, but because of whose you are."

"You are standing before Almighty God as an empty vessel, because you put to death on His cross, your identification of who and what He is, as well as what your identification of what love is."

(client repeats) "Come Holy Spirit, do Your job... fill this empty vessel with the wisdom, truth, knowledge, and character of Almighty God. I want to experience Your compassion, mercy, and grace. Now fill this empty vessel with the love of Almighty God ... pure, holy, and righteous love. Lord make me whole, so that I don't need anyone to fill an empty place in me. I put to death on your cross my need to be needed. Fill me with Your love to such overflowing that I can allow my husband/wife to be free to be themselves. He/she no longer has to perform to fulfill my desires or be what I need him/her to be, but rather he/she can give what he/she has, and I can receive it. I am whole and I am free to be myself, not what everyone expects me to be."

Lay hand on client's chest and pray:
(**PDM prays**) "God is reaching into your chest and squeezing your heart... and as He squeezes, your old identification of who and what He is and of what love is .. is being squeezed out of your heart. And as He releases ... like a sponge... you are absorbing the fullness of Almighty God. He is coursing Himself through every artery and every vein... every muscle, every tissue, every nerve ending. He is coursing Himself through every organ and every system in your body

... even into your mind where He is renewing your mind. He is coursing Himself through every ligament and every tendon, every sinew of your bone, every joint. And He is catching Himself up like fire in the marrow of your bone."

(client repeats) "Come Holy Spirit, wash the scales from my eyes, and allow me to see through Your eyes. Wash the blockage from my ears so that I can hear with Your ears Lord, and wash the stone from my heart, that I can love with Your heart. I give you my permission to knock down every wall that I have built to protect me from hurt. Shatter every inner vow I have ever made. (List any specific vows.)

(**PDM Prays**) Lord shatter every inner vow that your child has ever made and restore client to that perfect DNA blue print that You planned for him/her before the foundation of the world. client you are no longer required to act think or feel according to those inner vows. You are no longer required to run behind the walls, mazes, or masks. You are finally able to trust Father God and see Him as He really is a perfectly safe place in the time of trouble.

(client repeats) "Now Come Holy Spirit and fill the void that these bitter root judgments, bitter root expectations, signaling devices, restrictions, and antennas have left. Fill the void to overflowing with the fruit of the Spirit: love, joy, peace patience, kindness, goodness, faithfulness, gentleness, and self-control."

H. If client is an African American, Indian, etc., *repent and forgive for every white person who may have shown prejudice toward them. Repent for stealing their land, lying and breaking every promise made to them.*

I. Stand in as spiritual mom/dad:
(**PDM prays**) "I come before you as your spiritual mom and I repent for ... (list those things the client judged against mom).

"I come before you as your spiritual dad and I repent for ... (list those things the client judged against dad).

End by asking: "Can you forgive me for these things?"

"Can you say I forgive you mom?"
"Can you say I forgive you dad?"

When they do, hug them, bless them, tell them you love them.
In closing say: "Because you have forgiven, you can be forgiven. I speak forgiveness over you in the name of Jesus Christ. I call you into the fullness of your manhood/womanhood. I call your slumbering spirit to life in Jesus' name."

J. Sever Soul-Ties and Call In their Scattered, Fragmented Spirit:
(**PDM prays**) "We are about to sever off you every ungodly soul-tie. Ungodly soul ties are spiritual, emotional, physical, and sexual ties that you have made with anyone in your entire life ...
where they have used you or abused you in any of these areas. If there was fornication, adultery, or molestation, "you became one with those people outside of wedlock." "Their spirits are attached to you like tentacles pulling, drawing, and influencing ... and your spirit
has attached itself to them."

(Raise one hand above your head as you call in the client's spirit.
(**PDM prays**) "And now with the power that is in the name of Jesus Christ of Nazareth, I reach into the heavenlies and I am calling your spirit ..back to wholeness! (*Bring right hand down to client's forehead*) You are made whole and complete in Jesus' holy name!"

Important Note: This step by step outline is just that, an outline. It is not intended to be a formula. This is a Holy Spirit driven ministry and He will give you the direction in which you need to go. The above is a set of training wheels for you to get started on. We have found that these issues are the most common problems that our clients have dealt with. It is a composite of common issues we have seen since we started in this ministry. The prayers are only examples of what we do and how we do it. Use it as a guideline not an absolute.

Sample
Outline

Appendix B: The Homework

HOMEWORK FOR THE NEXT 31 DAYS

1. When a negative thought comes into your mind, say out loud:
 "THANK YOU LORD FOR TAKING CARE OF THAT."

You are saying 3 things when you say, "Thank you Lord for taking care of that."
- A. Lord, for the first time I am trusting that YOU will fight all of my battles.
- B. For the first time I take the fight out of me and lay it at the foot of the cross.
- C. For the first time in my life Lord, I am resisting the devil. I am not rebuking him, renouncing him, or casting him away. I am simply ignoring him. Thank you Lord for taking care of that.

2. When a negative word comes out of your mouth:
Say out loud, "CANCEL,
 I used to think that way,
 I used to feel that way,
 I used to be that way, but not anymore,
 Thank you Lord for taking care of that."

3. Each night before bed and each morning before you get up say out loud:
 I CHOOSE THIS DAY TO TRUST IN GOD!
 I choose life! I choose life! I choose life!
 I choose blessings! I choose blessings! I choose blessings!

I choose to walk in:

GOD'S LOVE	-	GOD'S PEACE
GOD'S JOY	-	GOD'S GLORY
GOD'S WISDOM	-	GOD'S HOPE
GOD'S FAVOR	-	GOD'S STRENGTH
GOD'S COURAGE	-	GOD'S PROSPERITY

When Emotions and Feelings Overwhelm You:
Remember that emotions and feelings are part of the autonomic nervous system, like blinking and breathing. You cannot control them you can only direct them. You don't want to stuff your feelings because they will find a way to the surface sooner or later, usually in a self-destructive manner. There are NO unexpressed emotions. The best thing to do is: Own them, to disown them. Say, "Lord, I take these emotions and feelings, (name them i.e., fear, rage, shame, blame, guilt, lust, unforgiveness, low self-esteem, etc) and I put them to death on your cross. Now come Holy Spirit and give me a glorious opposite. In my weakness is your strength"

These emotions and feelings are habits, patterns and structures. They are our Egypt. The Israelites cried so desperately to be free, and after only three (3) days they wanted to go back to Egypt. Why, because Egypt was so wonderful? NO. It was familiar. Sometimes, because of fear of the new walk, we will take familiar over freedom, even if the familiar was bad.

When you take in bitterness, anger, hurt, and unforgiveness, it is like you drinking poison waiting for someone else to die. If someone has caused you hurt, anger, or offense, you absolutely have a right to these emotions, and feelings. And you MUST say ouch. Share with that person or persons, that they offended and or hurt your feelings. This sets you free from allowing the offense to be stuffed and fester, but if you entertain the above offense, pride can and will sneak in the back door. God can do nothing, but push down the proud. A humble
person is not easily offended. You humble yourself by putting anger, hurt, and offense to death on the cross.

When you give up your right to these, God will exalt you, and even prepare a table before you in the presence of your enemies. It is better to be exalted by God than honored by man.

The Enemy Doesn't Want You to Walk Free!
The enemy will try to convince you that this kind of freedom isn't real, that nothing has changed and that everything is the way it was. You have to understand that Satan is the accuser of the brethren. It's his job to throw your failings, shortcomings, and sins in your face. He does this to drive you away from Father God.

Don't let him. When the enemy starts dredging up the past, starts giving you all the reasons you "can't get before God" let him. Then take all of those accusations, turn to your Heavenly Father and admit them; Confessing, repenting and receiving your forgiveness.
"THANK YOU LORD FOR TAKING CARE OF THAT."

Cleansing / Covering Prayer
To be used whenever you have been around defiling influences or places:

"Heavenly Father, cleanse my mind, body, soul, and spirit from all defilement. Scour the three levels of my mind Lord, the conscious, sub-conscious, and even unconscious levels with your cleansing blood. I take every thought captive to the obedience of Christ. Give me the mind of Christ Lord.

Father, hide me in the cleft of your rock, under the shadow of your wings. You are a strong tower, the righteous run into and are safe, and you have called me righteous. Blind the enemy as you did at Sodom so they can't even find an entrance into my life, physically, financially, emotionally, or spiritually in Jesus holy name."

Made in United States
Orlando, FL
08 January 2023